EUROPECOIN

A BORDERLESS BLOCKCHAIN

2014-2015-2016
A CONCISE EUROPECOIN HISTORY BOOK

Europecoin—A Borderless Blockchain

by Christopher P. Thompson

ISBN—13: 978-1548349929
ISBN—10: 1548349925

EUROPECOIN

A BORDERLESS BLOCKCHAIN

2014-2015-2016
A CONCISE EUROPECOIN HISTORY BOOK

CHRISTOPHER P. THOMPSON

CONTENTS

INTRODUCTION

Since the inception of Bitcoin in 2008, thousands of cryptocurrencies or decentralised blockchains have been launched. Most ventures into the crypto sphere have not gone to plan as their founders would have hoped. Nevertheless, there are currently hundreds of crypto related projects which are succeeding.

This book covers the history of Europecoin, an open-source, publicly accessible blockchain, from the 3rd May 2014 to the end of 2016. During that time, the project was rescued in late 2014 (original founder left) and a new blockchain was launched on the 8th July 2016. Since that time, development has been ongoing. Major topics covered in this book include:

- Announcement of Europecoin on the 3rd May 2014.

- Timestamping algorithm became pure proof of stake on the 19th May 2014.

- Europecoin abandoned for roughly six months between June and Dec 2014.

- Europecoin announced as taken over on the 21st December 2014.

- Market cap above US$100,000 for the first time on the 15th July 2015.

- An exchange called Comkort closed on the 20th July 2015.

- A hard fork of the blockchain occurred at block number 820,000 (original blockchain) on the 16th December 2015.

- A new blockchain (dubbed V3) was launched on the 8th July 2016.

- Users were able to swap their old V2 ERC for new V3 ERC.

- An all time high 2016 market capitalisation was attained in October 2016.

- An updated promotional video published on the 9th December 2016.

INTRODUCTION

This book covers thirty two (32) months, contained within six chapters, of historical events in chronological order. For six months between June and December 2014, the coin was abandoned.

You may have bought this book because Europecoin is your favourite cryptographic blockchain. Alternatively, you may be keen to find out how it all began. I have presented the information henceforth without going into too much technical discussion about Europecoin. If you would like to investigate further, I recommend that you read material currently available online at the official website at https://www.europecoin.eu.org/.

If you choose to purchase a certain amount of ERC, please do not buy more than you can afford to lose.

Enjoy the book :D

WHAT IS EUROPECOIN?

Europecoin is a cryptocurrency or digital decentralised currency used via the Internet. It is described as a payment network without the need for a central authority such as a bank or other central clearing house. It allows the end user to store or transfer value anywhere in the world with the use of a personal computer, laptop or smartphone. Cryptography has been implemented and coded into the network allowing the user to send currency through a decentralised (no centre point of failure), open source (anyone can review the code), peer-to-peer network. Cryptography also controls the creation of newly mined/minted ERC.

The Europecoin network protocol was created by using the source code inherent in Novacoin. As was the case with many cryptocurrencies launched in early 2014, the code of preceding coins was adopted and a few parameters were changed. After approximately two months, the original founder(s) abandoned the coin.

Europecoin was revitalised in late 2014 by Matthias Klees. He had spent five years working as a consultant for some of the European Commissioners in Brussels. He has been committed to the Europecoin project since he pursued its takeover.

On the official Europecoin website, the description of the coin is:

"Europecoin.eu.org is a currency and a workgroup-management platform, to manage expert teams and establish them as grassroots lobbying teams, in Europe. The website provides state of the art intranet-inspired communication and highly interconnected publishing, sharing and marketing tools, to support the teams, Their goal is, to educate decisionmakers about blockchain technology and to foster a "decentralization of powers" across Europe.

In this changing world, one day, even people presently in power, will have questions. They usually ask a lobby or "experts" around them. That's, why we would like to be around them too."

WHY USE EUROPECOIN?

Like all cryptocurrencies, people have chosen to adopt Europecoin as a medium of exchange through personal choice. An innovative feature of the coin, an affinity towards the brand or high confidence in the community could be reasons why they have done so. Key benefits of using Europecoin are:

- It is a useful medium of exchange via which value can be transferred internationally for a fraction of the cost of other conventional methods.

- Europecoin eliminates the need for a trusted third party such as a bank, clearing house or other centralised authority (e.g. PayPal). All transactions are solely from one person to another (peer-to-peer).

- Europecoin has the potential to engage people worldwide who are without a bank account (unbanked).

- Europecoin is immune from the effects of hyperinflation, unlike the current fiat monetary systems around the world.

Another interesting feature of the coin is the option to lock funds for a specific time (up to one year). It is known as the "Term Deposit". It rewards a stakeholder a percentage return depending on the time funds are held. Term deposits cannot be moved until the term ends. Five time periods exist:

1 month at ~3% p.a.   2 months at ~3.4% p.a.   3 months at ~4% p.a.

6 months at ~4.5% p.a.   1 year at ~5% p.a.

When a term deposit matures, it stops earning interest. It has to be moved to start earning interest again. Europecoin encourages saving.

IS EUROPECOIN MONEY?

Money is a form of acceptable, convenient and valued medium of payment for goods and services within an economy. It allows two parties to exchange goods or services without the need to barter. This eradicates the potential situation where one party of the two may not want what the other has to offer. The main properties of money are:

- **As a medium of exchange**—money can be used as a means to buy/sell goods/services without the need to barter.

- **A unit of account**—a common measure of value wherever one is in the world.

- **Portable**—easily transferred from one party to another. The medium used can be easily carried.

- **Durable**—all units of the currency can be lost, but not destroyed.

- **Divisible**—each unit can be subdivided into smaller fractions of that unit.

- **Fungible**— each unit of account is the same as every other unit within the medium (1 ERC= 1 ERC).

- **As a store of value**—it sustains its purchasing power (what it can buy) over long periods of time.

Europecoin easily satisfies the first six characteristics. Taking into account the last characteristic, the value of Europecoin, like all currencies, comes from people willing to accept it as a medium of exchange for payment of goods or services. As it gets adopted by more individuals or merchants, its intrinsic value will increase accordingly.

COIN SPECIFICATION

Since the birth of Europecoin, its coin specification has changed a few times. At the time of publication of this book, its current specification is:

Coin Symbol:	ERC
Unit of Account:	ERC
Date of Announcement:	3rd May 2014 at 21:43:51 UTC.
Date of Original Launch:	10th May 2014 at 16:00 UTC
Block Number One Generated:	8th July 2016 at 23:25:37 UTC (V3 Blockchain)
Founder:	User "EuropeCoin"
Lead Developer:	User "Limx Dev"
Hashing Algorithms:	HLOD (1GB ARS Pattern)
Timestamping Algorithm:	Hybrid proof of work and proof of stake.
Address Begins With:	E
Total Coins:	32,400,000 ERC (in approx. 15 years)
Block Time:	300 seconds
Reward Halving:	None
Difficulty Retarget Algorithm:	Dual KGW3
PoW Block Reward:	1 ERC
Pre-mine:	9,604,959 ERC (the majority were sent to users during the swap period)

MILESTONE TIMELINE

3rd May 2014	—Europecoin announced on Bitcointalk forum
7th May 2014	—User "minersmafia23" won the logo competition
10th May 2014	—The original blockchain was launched at 16:00 UTC
10th May 2014	—Bittrex initiated the trading pair ERC/BTC
10th May 2014	—Coin-Swap.net added both ERC/BTC and ERC/DOGE
11th May 2014	—Europex initiated the trading pair ERC/BTC
15th May 2014	—ShareXcoin initiated the trading pair ERC/BTC
18th May 2014	—First promotional video was unveiled on YouTube
19th May 2014	—Timestamping algorithm became pure PoS
5th June 2014	—Comkort initiated trading of Europecoin against Bitcoin, Litecoin and Dogecoin
27th June 2014	—Bittrex delisted Europecoin from their exchange
21st December 2014	—A new Bitcointalk thread was created in order to signify that the coin had been taken over.
23rd December 2014	—Twitter account created by Matthias Klees at http://twitter.com/europecoinEUORG
2nd March 2015	—First official ERC giveaway since the takeover
19th May 2015	—First Bitcoin Garden article written about the coin
19th May 2015	—Daily trading volume exceeded 1 BTC on Comkort
2nd June 2015	—Imminent closure of Comkort announced
15th June 2015	—Bleutrade initiated live trading of the pair ERC/BTC
18th June 2015	—Europecoin added to www.conimarketcap.com
29th June 2015	—Market capitalisation of the coin surpassed US$50,000 for the first time ever

MILESTONE TIMELINE

1st July 2015	—Trading ceased on Comkort at 18:00 UTC
4th July 2015	—A developer called Alberto was hired
15th July 2015	—Market capitalisation of the coin surpassed US$100,000 for the first time
16th July 2015	—Market capitalisation of the coin surpassed US$200,000 for the first time
17th July 2015	—Bittrex reintroduced the ERC/BTC trading pair
20th July 2015	—Comkort closed
25th July 2015	—Europecoin V2 pre-release announced
26th August 2015	—A coin logo design competition began
31st August 2015	—A payment provider called Cointopay began to support Europecoin
16th September 2015	—A new official Europecoin logo was unveiled
17th September 2015	—Europecoin added to the universal cloud staking service called Staisybit
8th October 2015	—Matthias announced a future hard fork
27th November 2015	—Number of accounts at Staisybit surpassed 100
16th December 2015	—Version two Windows wallet client released
21st December 2015	—First year anniversary of takeover celebrated
26th December 2015	—Version two Mac OS X wallet client released
17th February 2016	—AlcurEX initiated the trading pair ERC/BTC
19th February 2016	—Europecoin featured on the Bitcoin Rush Show
1st March 2016	—A developer called Infernoman came on board
30th March 2016	—A developer called user "Limx Dev" came on board

MILESTONE TIMELINE

3rd April 2016	—A logo was created by user "logocreator" for the "Federated Blockchains Initiative"
18th June 2016	—A shift to a new blockchain was proposed
20th June 2016	—Version 2.0.3 Windows wallet client released
22nd June 2016	—Version 2.0.3 Mac OS X wallet client released
5th July 2016	—Version 3 alpha wallet clients (testnet) released
8th July 2016	—Version 3 Windows wallet client released
8th July 2016	—New blockchain launched at 23:25:37 UTC
10th July 2016	—Version 3.0.1.0 wallet clients released (mandatory)
5th August 2016	—Version 3.0.1.1 Windows wallet client released
10th October 2016	—Android mobile wallet app released
21st October 2016	—One unit of ERC account surpassed 10,000 BTC Sat
22nd October 2016	—All time high 2016 market capitalisation was recorded at approximately US$857,642
31st October 2016	—Last official chance to swap V2 ERC for V3 ERC
9th December 2016	—New promotional video for the coin published
27th December 2016	—Version 3.0.2.0 wallet clients released
28th December 2016	—Version 3.0.2.0 Android mobile app released
31st December 2016	—Last block of the year timestamped at 23:53:54 UTC
31st December 2016	—Market capitalisation recorded at ~US$308,393

PROOF OF WORK (PoW) MINING

Proof of work mining is a competitive computerised process which helps to maintain and secure the blockchain in such a way as to verify transactions and prevent double spending.

In the general sense of cryptocurrency, those who participate in the activity of mining are called miners. They are general members of the cryptocurrency community who dedicate processing power (hash) of their computers towards solving highly complex mathematical problems and verifying transactions. This process upholds the integrity and security of the network. As such, miners are described as protectors of the network. Each transaction (held within a certain block) is validated before adding it to the blockchain. By doing this, they are rewarded (as an incentive) with newly generated mined coins or transaction fees. These coins are issued by the software in a transparent and predictable way outside of the control of its founders and developers. A miner can be based anywhere in the world as long as they have an internet connection, sufficient knowledge of how one mines and the hardware/software required to do so.

Miners use GPUs (Graphical Processing Units) or CPUs (Central Processing Units) to process transactions by hashing. Also, Application Specific Integrated Circuits (ASICs) allow miners to use customised hardware for faster and lower power mining.

Europecoin was hybrid proof of work for the first nine days of its existence. It then became pure proof of stake on the 19th May 2014. Since the new blockchain launched on the 8th July 2016, both PoW and PoS timestamping have been working side by side.

Proof of stake timestamping rewards wallet client users a certain annual percentage return if they keep their coins maturing for a specific time period.

BLOCKCHAIN

Every cryptocurrency has a corresponding blockchain within its decentralised network protocol. Europecoin is no different in this sense. A blockchain is simply described as a general public ledger of all transactions and blocks ever executed since the very first block. In addition, it continuously updates in real time each time a new block is successfully mined. Blocks enter the blockchain in such a manner that each block contains the hash of the previous one. It is therefore utterly resistant to modification along the chain since each block is related to the prior one. Consequently, the problem of doubling-spending is solved.

Two blockchains have served the Europecoin project. Originally, the first blockchain launched on the 10th May 2014. A new blockchain launched on the 8th July 2016 (rewritten protocol parameters and number of ERC reduced by a factor of ten).

As a means for members of the general public to view the blockchain, web developers have designed and implemented block explorers. They tend to present different layouts, statistics and charts. Some are more extensive in terms of the information given. Usual statistics included are:

- **Height of block**   —the block number of the network.

- **Time of block**   —the time at which the block was timestamped to the blockchain.

- **Transactions**   —the number of transactions in that particular block.

- **Total Sent**   —the total amount of cryptocurrency sent in that particular block.

- **Block Reward**   —how many coins were generated in the block (added to the overall coin circulation).

BLOCK REWARD/TIME

The block time is the average time taken for the network to successfully generate a certain block either by proof of work or proof of stake. Both the reward per block and the time of block generation dictate how the circulation of coins grows over time.

On the 8th July 2016, block number one of the new blockchain generated a total of 9,604,959 ERC. It was officially considered a pre-mine, but the vast majority of these were given out to users who participated in the swap in the summer/autumn of 2016. Official documents state that it takes an average of 300 seconds to find a block, but it does not differentiate between a PoW or PoS block.

DUAL Kimoto Gravity Well 3 is the retargeting resulting from KGW3 (in Bitsend) joined with a second virtual, hardcoded retarget, To stabilize the diff adjusting. in nearly realtime.It increases the diff, if the blocktarget hits more then blocktime/5 earlier, than standart Blocktime, (BT<SBT-SPT/5) by adding 15% and increasing dual diff. On the other side, it makes Bitbreak (our keep-blockchain moving microminer), to jump in immediately, in case of a hash down-swing this diff is moving virtually in real-time. The outcome, of this mechanism is breath taking, THIS ENGINE is lightening fast, precise like clockwork, rock stable but with realtime dynamics.
IT TAKES RAM / CPU MINING TO THE NEXT LEVEL.   WHATCHOUT!

A difficulty re-targeting algorithm called DUAL KGW3 is currently used to regulate the creation of blocks. When the processing power committed by miners increases, the difficulty is increased accordingly. This helps to maintain, as much as possible, the average 300 second block time. In addition, a mechanism called Bitbreak was introduced in case the processing power decreased/increased too quickly. Developers are constantly striving to improve upon difficulty re-targeting code.

From the launch of the new blockchain on the 8th July 2016 to the end of 2016, the number of ERC generated increased from 9,604,959 ERC to 9,713,368.05 ERC. This was a 1.129% increase over that time. It is a projected increase of 2.340% over an entire year.

CRYPTOCURRENCY EXCHANGES

A cryptocurrency exchange is a site on which registered users can buy or sell Europecoin against Bitcoin, Litecoin, Dogecoin and so on. Some exchanges require users to fully register by submitting certain documentation including proof of identity and address. On the other hand, most exchanges only require users to register with a simple username and password with the use of a currently held e-mail account.

As well as being the method by which people can buy or sell ERC, exchanges serve the purpose of setting the value of the coin. One unit of ERC account has always been valued in terms of Bitcoin Satoshi (1 BTC Sat = 0.00000001 BTC). A direct trade between fiat (USD, GBP, EUR) and Europecoin has never been available.

Bittrex was the first cryptocurrency exchange to initiate live trading of Europecoin against Bitcoin. This happened on the 10th May 2014. It delisted the coin on the 27th June 2014 because it was deemed a low volume trading pair. Over one year later, it was reinstated on the 17th July 2015. Bittrex is the only recognised exchange on which Europecoin trades today.

Other exchanges which offered its users the ability to trade ERC, but have since removed it, were:

EXCHANGE	STATUS
Coins-Swap.net	Closed
Europex	Closed
ShareXcoin	Closed
BetaShareX	Closed
Comkort	Closed
AlcurEX	Open
Bleutrade	Open

COMMUNITY

A community is a social unit or network that shares common values and goals. It derives from the Old French word "comuntee". This, in turn, originates from "communitas" in Latin (communis; things held in common). Europecoin has a community consisting of an innumerable number of individuals who have the coin's well being and future goal at heart. These individuals almost always prefer fictitious names with optional corresponding "avatars". Notable members of the community are Matthias Klees, user "metamorphin", user "Limx Dev" etc.

At the time of publication, there are social media sites (and other official websites) on which discussion and development of Europecoin take place. These are:

- https://europecoin.eu.org   (Official Website)

- https://chainz.cryptoid.info/erc   (Block explorer)

- https://twitter.com/europecoinEUORG   (Official Twitter Account)

Since the 21st December 2014, the following has been the official Europecoin Bitcointalk forum thread:

- https://bitcointalk.org/index.php?topic=901605.0

People usually check the market capitalisation and other associated metrics of the coin at:

- https://coinmarketcap.com/currencies/europecoin

In essence, the community surrounding and participating in the development of Europecoin is the backbone of the coin. Without a following, the prospects of future adoption and utilisation are starkly limited. Europecoin belongs to all those who use it, not just to the developers who aid its progression.

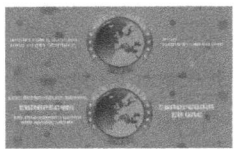

A CONCISE HISTORY OF EUROPECOIN

I.   **EUROPECOIN ANNOUNCED ON THE 3RD MAY 2014**

II.   **ORIGINAL COIN LOGO DESIGNED BY USER "MINERSMAFIA23"**

III.   **ORIGINAL BLOCKCHAIN WAS LAUNCHED ON THE 10TH MAY**

IV.   **BITTREX INITIATED ERC/BTC TRADING ON THE 10TH MAY**

V.   **COMKORT INITIATED TRADING OF ERC ON THE 5TH JUNE**

1

EUROPECOIN ANNOUNCED
ON BITCOINTALK

"Europe is a <u>*continent*</u> *that comprises the westernmost part of* <u>*Eurasia*</u>*. Europe is bordered by the* <u>*Arctic Ocean*</u> *to the north, the* <u>*Atlantic Ocean*</u> *to the west, and the* <u>*Mediterranean Sea*</u> *to the south. The eastern boundary with Asia is a historical and cultural construct, as there is no clear physical and geographical separation between them"* - Wikipedia

As is almost always the case, an official Bitcointalk forum thread was created for Europecoin at 21:43:51 UTC on the 3rd May 2014. A user simply known fictitiously as "EuropeCoin" created the thread, but it is unknown whether s/he was a lone individual or group of people. It was given the title "[ANN][ERC] EuropeCoin - Stabilization Fund - INNOVATIVE PoW/PoS SYSTEM"

On the 3rd May, the Europecoin team scheduled a tentative launch of the blockchain to occur on the 9th May at 22:00 UTC. Two exchanges called Bittrex and Comkort said they would support trading of ERC after the blockchain went live.

Other forums on which discussion and updates could be posted were founded in the next twenty four hours. Two officially recognised websites created straight after the announcement were the Twitter page https://twitter.com/EuropeCoinERC and the main website http://europe-coin.com.

During the first twenty four hours since the announcement, a coin logo competition began. User "EuropeCoin", the founder, encouraged eager designers to submit their proposals within the next three days. He wanted the design to look professional, but not too complicated. A theme of Europa in mythology and Europe as a union of borderless countries was sought after. A big bounty was promised for the winner. Some of the most favourable coin logo designs submitted were:

user "unlock.mk" (all five above)

user "Dmann" (two above) **user "minersmafia23"**

User "EuropeCoin" was amazed and impressed straight after the design by user "minersmafia23" was posted on the 4th May at 17:24:21 UTC.

The founder wanted a fair and transparent launch. A fast proof of work (PoW) period was planned followed by pure proof of stake (PoS) with dedicated multipool support. He also planned to release the wallet clients several minutes before launch in password protected zip files. An overview of the coin specification was:

- A total coin limit of 741 million ERC (est. population of Europe in 2014).

- A block target time of 60 seconds (average).

- A difficulty retargeting time of 60 seconds.

- A total of 137,547,000 ERC mined during the PoW phase.

- Hybrid PoW/PoS timestamping until PoW ceased at block number 20,160.

Proof of work mining was scheduled to last two weeks (approx. 20,160 blocks by taking into account the 60 second average block time). What follows is the initial block distribution table showing the rewards per block:

First Block	Last Block	# Blocks	Reward	Total	Cumulative
1	770	770	100	77,000	77,000
771	1,440	670	1,000	670,000	747,000
1,441	10,080	8,640	10,000	86,400,000	87,147,000
10,081	20,160	10,080	5,000	50,400,000	137,547,000

ERC block reward reduced from 10,000 ERC to 5,000 ERC on the 16th May.

The initial 770 blocks were set lower as a means to reduce the magnitude of a large proportion of coins being mined by a small group of early miners. An instamine of coins was being mitigated to a certain extent.

Besides the proof of work rewards, there were certain proof of stake minting rewards for wallet users who held ERC. These rewards varied during the first few weeks. Discrepancies existed to what the exact percentage figure returns were. After block number 20,160, the blockchain would become pure proof of stake.

On the 5th May, Comkort added Europecoin to their list of potential coin additions at https://comkort.com/vote#ERC. On the following day, another exchange called Bittrex pledged to initiate live trading of ERC against BTC on the 10th May.

On the 7th May at 12:20:00 UTC, user "minersmafia23" was announced as the winner of the coin logo design competition. He subsequently received the 25,000 ERC bounty for his successful entry (see page 24). Other participants were also rewarded smaller amounts of ERC.

On the 10th May at 16:00 UTC, the original blockchain launched. It was supposed to be launched the day before, but issues with the code delayed it. The developer wanted to be certain of a properly functioning network protocol. Shortly after launch, the first block explorer at http://explorer.europe-coin.com/ went live and the total limit of ERC to be minted was decreased to 384 million.

There were several cryptocurrency exchanges which initiated trading of Europecoin on their platforms in May. These were:

- On the 10th May, Bittrex initiated the trading pair ERC/BTC at https://bittrex.com/Market/?MarketName=BTC-ERC. They are based in Seattle, WA and fully regulated in the United States of America. They began operations on the 13th February 2014 in beta testing mode. On the 28th February 2014, twelve cryptocurrencies went live as trading became active.

- On the 10th May, Coin-Swap.net added ERC/BTC and ERC/DOGE.

- On the 11th May, an exchange called Europex initiated trading of ERC against BTC at https://www.europex.eu/#coin/btc/erc.

- On the 15th May, an exchange called ShareXcoin initiated trading of ERC against BTC at https://sharexcoin.com/market/ERC_BTC.

On the 18th May, the first Europecoin promotional video was unveiled on YouTube. It was simply titled "europecoin". It was uploaded by "Mark Satoshi", directed by Ouriel Benaroch and Michaël Harroch created the music. It ran for 48 seconds. A second promotional video was released within hours due to grammatical errors discovered in the original. Some screenshots of the video were:

On the 19th May, the timestamping algorithm switched to pure proof of stake. A quote derived from the original Europecoin Twitter account read:

"#EuropeCoin is now pure PoS!!! Enjoy your interest rate! No more direct mining for ERC! PoW finished! #ERC is now only PoS! at about 9 PM GMT on 19th May 2014."

It was noted that the number of coins mined/minted during the hybrid PoW/PoS phase had not reached or exceeded the planned 137,547,000 ERC. This was most likely due to the fact that a proportion of the blocks between 1 and 20,160 were PoS blocks. Unfortunately, the original developer did not make this clear. Instead, a coin circulation of approximately 93,800,000 ERC was the case.

During the last week of May, concerns began to grow that Europecoin would get delisted from Bittrex. Trading of Europecoin had descended to a very low daily trading volume. The initial founder(s) reiterated their commitment to the coin. They asked the community which features they wanted to see implemented.

On the 1st June, supporters were still voting to get Europecoin listed on the exchange called Comkort. Europecoin had 2,603 votes and was behind GlobalBoost (3,043 votes). Four days later, Comkort initiated three separate live trading pairs of Europecoin against Bitcoin, Litecoin and Dogecoin.

https://comkort.com/market/trade/erc_btc
https://comkort.com/market/trade/erc_ltc
https://comkort.com/market/trade/erc_doge

Over the following weeks, user "EuropeCoin" had become less responsive to questions and comments posted by the community. There were long periods during which time he did not submit a Bitcointalk forum thread post. Matthias Klees began to participate in the community in early June. He was investigating the potential of the coin and kept track of development progress. He was becoming demoralised about the way in which the coin was heading.

Bittrex listed Europecoin for removal on the 27th June. Daily trading volume was below 0.1 BTC and one unit of ERC account had descended to a value of two Bitcoin Satoshi (0.00000002 BTC). A gloomy future for the coin seemed likely.

    I.   **EUROPECOIN TAKEN OVER ON THE 21ST DECEMBER 2014**

    II.   **MATTHIAS KLEES SEARCHED FOR A TALENTED DEVELOPER**

    III.   **IMMINENT CLOSURE OF COMKORT ANNOUNCED**

    IV.   **BLEUTRADE INITIATED TRADING OF ERC ON THE 15TH JUNE**

    V.   **ERC ADDED TO WWW.COINMARKETCAP.COM**

2

TAKEOVER OF

EUROPECOIN

"Europecoin is not a brand new coin. It is indeed a successful example of community takeover. The primary mission of the coin is to educate people within the EU community."

On the 21st December 2014, a new Bitcointalk forum thread was created in order to signify that Europecoin had been taken over. A fresh direction was required to take the coin forward. Matthias Klees, or user "szenekonzept", had become the main point of contact and was willing to revitalise the community. His first task was to assess the health of the blockchain. It was vital that there were still users who were staking/minting ERC. The original specification from the founder still stood. It was noted that the vast majority of trading was occurring on Comkort. Bittrex delisted the coin in spring/summer 2014.

Two days later, a new Twitter account was created and announced by Matthias Klees at http://twitter.com/europecoinEUORG . It is still active today.

Any programmers who liked the proposed ideas, scope and direction of Europecoin were encouraged to contact Matthias Klees.

As previously mentioned, Europecoin had simply been taken over, not hard forked. The original specification still stood and initial coin holders still had their ERC. Matthias Klees wanted to search for as many "like-minded" individuals as possible who favoured the idea of a decentralised Europe through building grassroot lobby groups. He also sought development of the coin to follow the wishes of its users. At this early stage, he knew progress would be slow. One major objective at the time was to contact payment providers. A broad definition of a PP is:

"It offers shops online services for accepting electronic payments by a variety of payment methods including credit card, bank-based payments such as direct debit, bank transfer, and real-time bank transfer based on online banking."

On the 26th January, a short summary of what had happened during the past month was published. A campaign was being planned to get supporters/followers involved with recruiting merchants. Another idea proposed was to implement a poll management service. It would give members of the community a better voice.

At the end of January, the network protocol was running as expected. A node had been established in order for blocks to be found successfully via staking.

On the 10th February at 01:49:58 UTC, the image below and a corresponding comment were posted on the official Europecoin Bitcointalk thread. Matthias Klees was pleased to have witnessed that the Bitcoin Satoshi value of one unit of ERC account had recovered. It had reached 69 Bitcoin Satoshi or 0.00000069 BTC.

As the month of February progressed, discussions continued to take place as to how best move the coin forward. Other cryptocurrency teams praised the commitment and effort of Matthias Klees. On the 14th February, user "cryptonit" praised the concept/objective of ERC by saying it could "go very far". Matthias thanked him and was keen to know his opinion on other issues. This was the first notable sign of friendship and collaboration between the Diamond and Europecoin development teams. Matthias was very impressed by the recent updates posted in the Diamond community. Diamond, DMD, was launched on the 13th July 2013 at 06:22:11 UTC by user "JohnLuc". Its market capitalisation reached US$5.918 million on the 6th June 2017. A maximum coin total of 4,380,000 DMD is specified.

Other events which occurred during the month of February were:

- After monitoring the exchange called BetaShareX, Matthias Klees removed links to it from the official ERC Bitcointalk thread. There had been issues with missing deposits. Comkort was recommended as the best alternative.

- Matthias Klees was busy moving office at the end of the month. He moved his office to Bochum, Germany.

On the 2nd March, the first official ERC giveaway since the take over began. A sum of 100 ERC would be sent to each supporter who retweeted a ERC related tweet.

Throughout the remaining weeks of March, an eight week campaign plan was put forward. Key points to focus on were:

- Attracting the expertise to develop/compile the next wallet clients.

- Get ERC added to a multipool to support the strength of the ERC network.

- Motivate the community via "game like" giveaways (when ERC reaches certain milestone goals).

- Push for frequent press releases to support the campaign.

On the 10th April, there were concerns the coin had been abandoned. Matthias responded by saying Europecoin was "very alive". He said he had been experimenting with code on Github for the first time. He admitted that the project was behind schedule. He emphasised that the core Europecoin team only consisted of himself for the time being. He was quoted as saying:

"This is a one-man-show, so expect things to move in an laid back manner."

He advised members of the community to read the opening page of the Europecoin Bitcointalk thread and reached out to the wider crypto sphere for help.

On the 28th April, Matthias moved the source code from his personal repository to a organisation repository. Some bounties were also announced on this day:

1)   Windows Binary from the current Git-Repository 15000 ERC

2)   Mac Binary from the current Git-Repository 15000 ERC

3)   Teaching Matthias how to compile a Windows Binary 25000 ERC

4)   Multipool to mine ERC (can also keep the pool fee) 250 000 ERC

The first giveaway campaign that began on the 2nd March was still active.

On the 14th May at 21:45:18 UTC, it was noted that the Bitcoin Satoshi value of one ERC unit of account had reached 94 Bitcoin Satoshi. Taking into account that one Bitcoin was worth roughly US$238 on this day, one ERC equated to US$0.00022372.

On the 19th May, an article was published on Bitcoin Garden (a social Bitcoin/ altcoin news network website) titled "EuropeCoin: A Movement to Decentralize Europe". It described the primary objective of Europecoin as an effort to educate the people of Europe about the benefits of blockchain technology. Questions were expected from individuals and groups. Matthias Klees was quoted as saying:

"Our organization aims to find people, that are interested and competent enough,
to develop expert groups and use the time to mature, learn and finally function in a way,
that will be needed in Brussels."

Furthermore, the article made reference to the principal exchange, Comkort, on which Europecoin was being traded on. Three trading pairs were still active (against BTC, LTC and DOGE). Matthias Klees was also quoted as saying:

"So I wanted to build a piece of technology, that's not necessarily a technological
innovation, but provides a tool for the community, to do the groundwork: To find answers
them self and maybe THEN scripting those answers into Blockchains or whatever."

Matthias had also contacted several magazines and he expected to see more articles on Bitcoin Garden (https://bitcoingarden.org).

Also on the 19th May, the daily trading volume of Europecoin on Comkort went above 1 BTC. The BTC Satoshi value of one unit of ERC account had reached 322. A chart derived from Comkort depicts this:

On the 2nd June, there was unfortunate news. User "gaazje" notified the community of the imminent closure of Comkort. The Comkort press release read:

"Regretfully we have to inform you that Comkort exchange is ceasing operation. Throughout the whole term of our existence we have strived to deliver an the best possible service for profitable cryptocurrency trading. And yet, the time has come to terminate our service.

In light of these event ALL users have to withdraw their funds before July 19th, 2015 inclusively. July 20th, 2015 we will suspend servers which will deactivate all the wallets and all further withdrawals will be technically impossible.

Trading will be stopped July 1st, 2015 at 18:00 GMT. All active orders will be cancelled."

Comkort stated the main reason for closing as simply not being able to stay profitable. If any users were having difficulty in withdrawing funds, they were prepared to help. Matthias Klees thanked Comkort for their honest service.

As a consequence of the imminent closure of Comkort, Matthias Klees initiated a 100,000 ERC reward bounty for anybody who could successfully get the coin active on another well known exchange. Cryptsy, Poloniex, Bittrex, Gatecoin, C-Cex, Bleutrade and others were suggested as possible options. It had been agreed that the next exchange would gain exclusive support from Europecoin.

On the 14th June, encouraging news broke. Europecoin had been added to Bleutrade following on from the successful campaign on Twitter. Bleutrade trading of ERC against BTC went online on the 15th June (active from this day). Matthias Klees said:

"WE DID IT AGAIN - GREATEST TEAM EVER this campaign was really fun!
Thank you to all the countless supporters out there, you created a thunderstorm.
Special thanks to Bitcoingarden and to Devnullius you both have a supporter out there.
Ask for anything at any time!"

Matthias was pleased that the lack of an exchange had been resolved. His prime focus was to return to the goal of acquiring trusted payment providers.

On the 18th June, Europecoin was finally added to www.coinmarketcap.com. They are an infamous website on which of vast majority of cryptocurrencies are listed in order of market capitalisation (the total value of all units of account).

On the 29th June, the market capitalisation of ERC was recorded above US$50,000 for the first time. It was ranked at 162 on www.coinmarketcap.com.

$ 0.000547 (68.00 %)
0.00000219 BTC (68.45 %)

Market Cap	Volume (24h)	Available Supply
$ 51,372	$ 47	93,845,753 ERC
206 BTC	0 BTC	

Matthias Klees promised updates/news in the next few days. He had been making contacts to help keep the project moving forward.

I. MARKET CAP SURPASSED US$100K FOR THE FIRST TIME

II. BITTREX REINSTATED THE ERC/BTC TRADING PAIR

III. EUROPECOIN VERSION TWO PRE-RELEASE ANNOUNCED

IV. CURRENT COIN LOGO UNVEILED

V. CLOUD STAKING SERVICE STAISYBIT BEGAN TO SUPPORT ERC

3

VERSION TWO WALLET
PRE-RELEASE ANNOUNCED

"Europecoin is continuing to work out several features to foster a currency, that enables a convenient and decentralised market activity for the future of Europe."

On the 3rd of July, a undisclosed ERC bounty was commissioned by Matthias in order to attract the attention of a developer. Matthias was not very technically apt to fully develop Europecoin to its fullest potential. In particular, he was searching for a developer who could upgrade the wallet client code. He was willing to hear from potential candidates inside and outside the cryptocurrency community.

It was not long until a developer agreed to help. A secretive person had been hired to look over the code and recommend improvements.

On the 5th July, Matthias was pleased to notify the community that an anonymous investor had bought a significant number of ERC. It was reported that the number of ERC bought to support the coin was unknown.

Matthias kept promising he would keep everyone updated as much as possible on Bitcointalk. Twitter was the most active platform for the coin.

On the 15th July, another milestone event occurred. The market capitalisation of Europecoin surpassed US$100,000 for the first time. One unit of ERC account reached an average value of 515 Bitcoin Satoshi (0.00000515 BTC). Taking into account that 1 Bitcoin was worth ~US$292 on this day, one ERC equated to ~US$0.0015038. In addition, a 10 BTC daily trading volume of ERC was attained.

On the following day, Europecoin entered the top hundred of cryptocurrencies listed on www.coinmarketcap.com. It had just surpassed a market capitalisation of US$200,000. This can be seen immediately below:

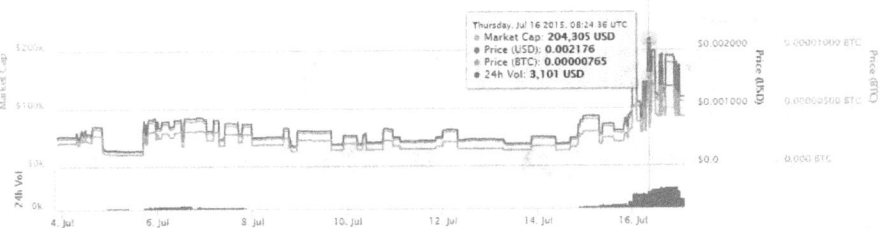

On the 17th July, news broke that Europecoin was back on Bittrex. Matthias hesitantly welcomed the relisting of the coin on Bittrex. He had wanted to wait for it. He still regarded Bleutrade as a sentimental exchange that rescued Europecoin.

On the 25th July, after several days of minor updates to the wallet clients, Matthias proudly presented the "Europecoin V2 Pre-release". An article was published by Bitcoin Garden on the same day. It described the new features. Special thanks were given to the new developer called Alberto who had shown commitment and had worked tirelessly to clear up some senseless code. New features included:

- An optimised VPOS staking engine (uses 75% less memory).

- Staking statistics and market statistics from Bittrex and Bleutrade.

- An in-wallet trading client.

Before the release, there were tests which still had to be carried out. They anticipated its release after the VPOS staking engine had passed block 10,000 on testnet. A warm welcome was given to user "metamorphin" who had recently joined the Europecoin team.

On the 2nd August, Matthias Klees issued a weekly report in which he gave his opinions on the value of Europecoin, the coin's future and current development news. He was relieved that the recent slump in the market capitalisation had } subsided since it went over US$200,000 in mid-July. One unit of ERC account was now valued at 219 Bitcoin Satoshi.

One particular idea proposed in early August was the concept of cloudstaking. In partnership with others, he had founded Bitcoinsulting, Cryptolab and Thinktank. A cloudstaking company was advantageous. Users would be able to easily move coins into the cloud, and vice versa, without those coins actually leaving the wallet. An in-wallet cloudstaking function was being investigated and developed.

In addition to the news above, Alberto notified Matthias that the test-run of the new VPOS staking engine was complete. It was now ready to find its way into the next major release. Other features were also being developed for inclusion.

A summary of the work in progress was:

- Talking to potential payment providers.

- Preparing for the release of version two of the ERC wallet clients.

- Preparing for the launch of their own service for in-wallet cloudstaking.

- Brainstorming ideas attaining to user experience on the official website at http://europecoin.eu.org. They wanted an increase in engagement.

On the 26th August, more information was released in connection to the ERC team buying into a cloudstaking company. It was scheduled to open within the next several weeks. Alberto had been tasked with developing the associated code. The name of the company was Staisybit and people were directed to register at https://staisybit.com. Testers were needed for the "open beta" system.

Also on the 26th August, a coin logo design competition was initiated. There was a feeling that the project required a new look/appearance to coincide with the next major release of the wallet client. Designs would be publicly posted to give members of the community the opportunity to express their opinions.

On the 31st August, it was announced that a "payment provider" called Cointopay had added and began to support EuropeCoin. Matthias viewed this as an important addition and was confident of further payment providers supporting Europecoin.

On the 14th September, a status summary was published. Europecoin had come a long way since it was taken over. It was time to make the coin stronger by adding valuable and independently created services to the ecosystem. Another objective was to grow the community. A framework for establishing a lobby for decentralisation was an ongoing venture. Key points of the vision were cited:

- Building an ecosystem independent from any institution, exchange or other service.

- Forming groups within countries which educate people and foster adoption.

- Training expert lobby groups.

- Create a consulting service in Brussels by establishing small educational events in the city.

- Actively engage with third parties to increase research and development.

On the 16th September, a new official logo was made available for publishers to use at their own discretion. This was:

On the 17th September at 13:00:04 UTC, user "StaisyBit" announced that Europecoin had been added to Staisybit, a new universal cloud staking wallet service. Users were now able to mint/stake ERC without having to resort to downloading the full blockchain on to their personal computers. At the time, the service was still in beta phase and withdrawals were temporarily disabled.

Towards the end of September, efforts were still ongoing to finalise the code of the next major release. It was expected in the next few weeks (depending on how well development progressed). The first staking tests on Staisybit were reported as a great success. Matthias Klees gave praise to the support from the Diamond community (DMD Foundation), Noble, Bitcoin Garden, Altcoin Today, Bleutrade and all users who had been helping too. He had no doubt that Europecoin would not have been as successful without their support.

I.   HARD FORK OCCURRED AT BLOCK NUMBER 820,000

II.   ONE YEAR SINCE THE SUCCESSFUL TAKEOVER

III.   ALCUREX INITIATED LIVE TRADING OF ERC

IV.   EUROPECOIN FEATURED ON THE BITCOIN RUSH SHOW

V.   IDEA OF A FEDERATED BLOCKCHAIN INITIATIVE WAS BORN

4

HARD FORK ANNOUNCEMENT

"In this changing world… (the) people… in power will have questions. They (will) ask "experts" around them. These "experts" are mostly lobbyists for paying corporations. That is why we would like to… provide another perspective." - Matthias Klees

In an ecstatic manner, Matthias Klees announced the future hard fork of the blockchain. He submitted a detailed post on the official Europecoin Bitcointalk thread on the 8th October at 22:02:51 UTC. Three months of programming from the developer at Staisybit, Alberto, had reached a point at which a working Windows wallet client was ready. Alberto was noted for kick starting development to the next level. In addition to the in-wallet trading and market statistic features in the pre-release, a new cloudstaking control tab had also been implemented.

Before the release of the ERC V2 wallet client, it was critical to run the new protocol parameters on testnet. It was viewed as vital to make sure of a smooth transition. Once again, the partnerships with other cryptocurrencies such as Diamond and Fuelcoin were celebrated. Matthias promised to keep the community informed of progress over the coming weeks and months ahead.

Most of the time in October was spent on how to proceed with the future hard fork of the blockchain. There were hardly any notable events which occurred, except for the addition of ERC to an automatic trader called CAT on the 29th October.

After a successful development and testing phase, the ERC V2 Windows wallet client was announced as released on the 16th December at 00:11:18 UTC. A major flaw in the code was fixed about 100 blocks before the 2,000 block target on testnet. Approximately twelve hours were given for both Bittrex and Bleutrade before the hard fork was scheduled to kick in at block number 820,000. Matthias was quoted as saying:

"After experiencing two weeks of thrilling events, we still stand stronger than ever. So we proudly present the real, the brand spanking new variance proof of stake engine with our even more spanking new security fixes. Upgrade mails sent to all newsletter subscribers."

Major features included in the release were as follows:

- Market statistic and graphs from Bittrex and Bleutrade.

- An in-wallet cloudstaking control centre.

- A new variance enabled V-POS staking written from scratch.

Proof of stake block rewards for the first eight weeks after block 820,000 were:

Week	Percentage p.a.	Week	Percentage p.a.
1	0.5	5	1.5
2	1	6	3
3	1	7	3
4	1.5	8	5

Europecoin was the product of a successful reboot of a former coin. A broad infrastructure had been built. Staisybit was founded primarily to help fund the project without relying on donations from the community. Another company called "Bitcoinsulting Group Europe" was also established to fund community members by freeing them to work for the project. They are willing to fund speeches or consulting ventures to spread the idea of decentralisation and blockchain across Europe, and perhaps, beyond. People across Europe were contributing to make Europecoin readily available in different countries. Ultimately, the message of the coin was constantly being broadcasted to aid higher adoption.

As had been customary for Europecoin, a graphic was unveiled to celebrate the first anniversary of the coin since the take over:

On the last day of 2015, the market capitalisation was recorded at US$139,464 according to www.coinmarketcap.com. Besides this figure, the US$ value of one unit of ERC account was roughly 0.00147 and the BTC Sat value of approximately 341. The market cap had not exceeded US$200,000 again since the 16th July 2015.

After New Year celebrations, there were hardly any updates from the official team. The first major event was that Europecoin had been integrated as a base coin for all coming ROKOS Flavour releases for IoT (Internet of Things) devices. Europecoin was one of a few preconfigured default coins on every device.

On the 10th January, user "OKtoshi" said he was honoured with the recently formed collaboration with Europecoin. He was quoted as saying:

"Congratulations to ERC for claiming a "Permanent add promo" showing Real commitment to their communities to support long term adoption."

OKCash is a separate cryptocurrency. Its blockchain launched on the 24th November 2014 at 21:39:38 UTC. Its market cap surpassed US$10,000,000 on the 10th June 2017. More information is available at http://okcash.co/.

On the 14th January, an upgrade to the previously released ERC V2 wallet client was released. It was a "bugfixed" version. Developers went through the code thoroughly and feedback was welcome.

Another mandatory upgrade was issued two weeks later. There had been problems with the staking mechanism. Matthias Klees was relieved that this particular upgrade had resolved the staking problems. A working Mac OS X wallet client was compiled and made available a few days later.

During the first week of February, promotion of Europecoin ramped up. A video artist was being sought after to create a great clip for ERC with a 80,000 ERC incentive bounty. On the 18th Febraury, the bounty increased to 150,000 ERC.

On the 17th February at 19:11:12 UTC, user "halibit" announced that ERC had just been integrated into the exchange called alcurEX at https://alcurex.org/index.php/crypto/market?pair=ERC_BTC. alcurEX is a cryptocurrency financing company registered in Finland. There were three recognised exchanges which allowed its users to actively trade Europecoin at this time.

On the 19th February, Europecoin featured on the Bitcoin Rush Show which can be watched on YouTube. It is described as a crypto news media show for the community. It has run for several years. The presenter spoke about how the coin was rescued, the services behind it and its future direction.

After being absent for a few days, Matthias returned to Bitcointalk. On the 1st March, another developer got on board to help look over the wallet client code. He was introduced as Infernoman (Transfercoin, Infernopool).

Work continued to improve the robustness and security of the network. User "metamorphin" praised the whole community and the ongoing achievements. He was quoted as saying:

"I love this coin, I love you community...My heart is always full with europecoin!"

On the penultimate day of March, yet another developer (user "Limx Dev") joined the team via cross collaboration from the cryptocurrency called Bitend. Bitsend was another cryptocurrency that was taken over. His insight into the code was viewed as amazing.

Two days prior to user "Limx Dev" joining the team, the market capitalisation exceeded US$200,000 for the first time since 16th July 2015.

As a consequence of the ever growing collaboration with cryptocurrencies such as Diamond, Bitsend, OKCash etc., the idea of a "Federated Blockchains Initiative" was born. It is described as a "crypto thinktank" to allow streamlined cross communication between different cryptocurrencies. Four developers had recently attended its first conference.

On the 3rd April, user "logocreator" published a logo (below) for the "Federated Blockchain Initiative". Matthias described user "logocreator" as the best designer of logos in the crypto community and recommended others to contact him.

After weeks of testing, another update to the wallet client was released on the 23rd April. The developers insisted that any bug/issues found got reported immediately so that they could be fixed. They were confident that the vast majority of issues had been ironed out. Praise was given to all those people, especially user "Limx Dev" (aka. Chris), who had contributed hundreds of hours. The stigma of a malfunctioning wallet was erased. A quote from user "metamorphin" was:

"Congratulation! My wallet is working perfect now with this newest installer. Chris, you are my hero now! :-D

I wanna praise the combination of a big enthusiastic community and the cooperations with different coins, applications and their leaders and developers; in our cause BITSEND, STAISYBIT, TRANSFERCOIN and a lot of infos from different more. (EDIT: Very special thanks also to the DMD-TEAM for discussing stuff in many hours) By the way, JOHN, I see also ERC in ur fooder. You are great."

On the 20th May, there were concerns about the very low daily trading volumes on the exchanges which were trading ERC. Matthias understood that more volume was needed on Bittrex, otherwise ERC would be delisted for the second time. A daily trading volume of at least 0.2 BTC was required on Bittrex. There was low volume on both Bleutrade and alcurEX too.

For the remaining ten days of May and the first three weeks of June, there were few updates from the core team and the number of posts on Bitcointalk by Matthias was slim. Matthias had been talking to several third parties to widen the appeal of Europecoin to a greater audience. Adoption remained the key to success over the long term.

Other events which occurred during this period were:

- On the 2nd November, UberPay announced the addition of Europecoin.

- On the 27th November, the number of registered accounts at Staisybit surpassed 100.

- From the 8th February, users were able to buy webhosting (see logo below) at https://cryptocloudhosting.org/ using ERC.

- On the 10th February, thanks to user "Woody20285", multipool mining for Europecoin was initiated at Inferno Pool.

I.   INNUMERABLE CODE VARIATIONS WERE BEING TESTED

II.   VERSION 2.03 WALLET CLIENTS RELEASED

III.   MATTHIAS EAGER TO HIRE MORE DEVELOPERS

IV.   ALPHA TESTNET CLIENT RELEASED ON THE 5TH JULY

V.   MAX NUMBER OF COINS TO REDUCE BY A FACTOR OF TEN

5

TRANSITION TOWARDS
A NEW BLOCKCHAIN

"Always doing the same thing over and over again and expecting a different outcome is the true insanity" - Albert Einstein

For the past several weeks, the developers had been busily thinking about changes to the coin specification and network protocol parameters. On the 18th June, Matthias shared his opinion on whether to replace sole PoS with HODL. (a sort of Ram-Mining Concept). Discussions ensued between notable figures in the team about how to create a new codebase. They wished to find out which course of action would best suit investors and attract new users.

Innumerable PoW/PoS timestamping variations were being tested to find the most favourable outcome. Matthias also promised to implement a feature called "Bitbreak". It jumps in if there are not enough miners to keep the chain moving.

Matthias, and the growing team besides him, wanted a fresh approach. He wanted to rethink the innovative style of Europecoin. He emphasised that his devotion to the project would not wane; he was relentless to see it succeed.

On the 20th June, in order to make the transition to the new blockchain smooth, an updated version (v2.03) of the Windows wallet client was released. A Mac OS X version was released two days later.

One week later, a new block explorer for the coin became fully operational at http://chain.blockpioneers.info/erc/explorer/.

As the month of June came to a close, further venture capitalist funds were disclosed as received. Another business partnership had recently been formed. Other developments reported were:

- Matthias was eager to hire more talented and professional developers.

- Hardware had already been obtained to develop a peer-2-peer point of sales cash system (touchscreen payment terminals).

Concerning the transition to the new blockchain, ideas were welcome on what the coin specification should be. Matthias had promised to keep the total coin count, but was prepared to change it if the community wanted.

A poll was created on the 30th June to help decide which direction to take. A lower coin reward per block was evidently desired.

Matthias Klees happily made an announcement about project operations moving to a new office on the 15th July. It would become the official address of the Europecoin project. He was well aware that the move would hamper his responsiveness of communications, but he was committed to respond to people within 24 hours. A photograph of an office sign was unveiled on the 2nd July:

On the 5th July, the alpha testnet version of the new blockchain was released. It was assessed as being stable and ready to be thoroughly tested. Matthias wanted members of the community to help test it too. Some of the new coin specification was:

- Five minute block time and Dual KGW difficulty retargeting algorithm.

- A static PoW block reward of 1 ERC after block number one (~1.04& p.a.)

- A PoS interest rate of ~2.48% p.a.

- An additional feature called "Term Deposit" had also been implemented (see page 11 for details).

On the following day, details emerged of how the community had voted regarding the future V3 coin specification. Agreement was viewed as radical:

a) Upgraded to the newest stable Bitcoin Core.

b) Will go back to PoW and will feature HODL RAM mining.

c) Will enable a timelock function for interest.

d) Will have Bitlock protection to keep the chain moving, even if there are no miners.

e) Will be swapped over a secure swap server, reducing total coins to 9.6 million and max supply to 32 million (ratio 10:1).

There was enthusiasm for a smooth, successful and satisfying transition. Once the developers knew the code was functioning how it should be, the full release was expected in the next few days. If anyone discovered problems if the alpha client, they were asked to report to the developers as soon as possible.

I.   **NEW V3 BLOCKCHAIN LAUNCHED ON THE 8TH JULY 2016**

II.   **USERS BEGAN TO SWAP OLD V2 ERC FOR NEW V3 ERC**

III.   **ALL TIME HIGH 2016 MARKET CAPITALISATION RECORDED**

IV.   **A NEW PROMOTIONAL VIDEO UPLOADED TO YOUTUBE**

V.   **MATTHIAS STILL DEVOTED TO THE EUROPECOIN PROJECT**

6

VERSION THREE
BLOCKCHAIN LAUNCHED

"EuropeCoin ERC3—We Adapt—We Always Move" - Matthias Klees

On the 8th July at 23:50:10 UTC, the Windows wallet release was made available by user "Limx Dev" (Christain) on the official Europecoin Bitcointalk thread. A new feature called "Term Deposit" was included.

Windows Wallet
https://dl.dropboxusercontent.com/u/21000833/ERC/ERC_3.0.0.0/europecoin-qt.exe

Source:
https://github.com/LIMXTEC/Europecoin-V3

A swap server at http://www.europecoin.eu.org/swap-tool-erc was going to be launched. It would allow users to easily convert their old V2 ERC and, in return, receive their new V3 ERC. The core team promised ample time for this. It would be the responsibility of user "Limx Dev" to transfer the coins manually every Monday.

For information purposes, the first nine blocks of the new blockchain had been timestamped before the announcement of the Windows wallet release on the 8th July. Including the tenth block, these were:

#	Time (UTC)	Reward (ERC)		#	Time (UTC)	Reward (ERC)
1	23:25:37	9,604,959		6	23:48:31	1
2	23:47:51	1		7	23:48:40	1
3	23:48:02	1		8	23:49:29	1
4	23:48:12	1		9	23:50:07	1
5	23:48:22	1		10	23:51:07	1

Instructions on how to transition from the old blockchain to the new blockchain were regularly posted by user "metamorphin". It was vital no one was left behind during this technical phase. He methodically went through the steps of how to proceed. He stressed the importance of transferring ERC from version 2.0.3.0 to the swap server. Other key points posted by user "metamorphin" were:

- Please create for every transaction a new withdraw address.
- Your received for 10 ERC one new ERC (10:1).
- The payout day for new ERCs is always Monday.
- The minimum amount is 250 old ERC.
- We pay only full new ERC (250.007 old ERC = 25 new ERC).

Users were advised not to panic. As promised, there was plenty of time for new V3 ERC to be acquired trouble free. Bittrex were not involved in the swap and would not be automatically swapping user's ERC on their exchange. However, this changed later on. A quote from user "metamorphin" at the time was:

"PRAISE our awesome developer team. We wouldnt be here, if Chris wouldnt go line for line through the unique code of ERC. We wouldnt be known, if Matthias wouldnt manage the marketing and lead the coin."

Block #1 (Reward 9,604,959 ERC) July 8th 2016 at 11:25:37 PM UTC

On the 10th July, a new mandatory Windows/Linux wallet client was released (version 3.0.1.0). It included a fix to the Dual KGW3 Bitbreak re-targeting algorithm. A Mac OS X release shortly followed.

On the following day, a non-mandatory (cosmetic) update was made available at https://github.com/LIMXTEC/Europecoin-V3/releases/tag/Europecoin_V3.0.1.0-2

On the 16th July, the first V3 block explorer had been created by user "BanzaiBTC" and was subsequently made accessible at http://chain.blockpioneers.info/erc/. The block explorer for the old blockchain was still active.

Saying that they were not going to beforehand, Bittrex notified the community that they had automatically swapped all user's ERC to new V3 ERC. As a result, user "Limx Dev" urgently warned people not to send ERC from Bittrex to Bleutrade. Bleutrade was still on the old blockchain.

On the 23rd July, problems persisted with people failing to realise that Bleutrade was still on the old V2 blockchain. This was causing "burned coins". Matthias Klees assured users that if they reported their burnt coin transactions, then they would still get their new V3 coins. It would take time, so users were asked to remain calm and patient.

Since the swap program began, a significant proportion of the conversation on the official Europecoin Bitcointalk thread involved users asking questions about how to update, where missing coins had gone and waiting for their V3 ERC coins (payments done in weekly batches for security reasons).

On the 5th August, version 3.0.1.1 Windows wallet client released.

On the 6th August, version 3.0.1.1 Mac OS X wallet released.

On the 15th August, a prominent member of the Diamond community called user "cryptonit" was quoted as saying:

"it would be fair to state early and clear a enddate of swap, i would suggest 31.12.2016
then we can close the chapter ERC v2 and concentrate all energies on ERC v3
also a clear statement that not claimed coins get burned should be made
this way we all can expect our ERC to become even more rare"

Matthias Klees said he would consider the recommendation, but wished to keep the swap open indefinitely. He wanted as many users to swap coins as possible. He did though, however, say he wanted the swap to be concluded by January 2017.

On the 25th August, Matthias rejoiced that the team working on the Europecoin project consisted of more than four highly productive, full time individuals. He pointed out the team had not come together by chance, but was the result of careful selection during the preceding months.

On the following day, a second block explorer was up and running for the new V3 ERC blockchain at https://chainz.cryptoid.info/erc/.

By the end of August, the first post of the official Europecoin Bitcointalk thread had been updated to include as much information about the recent changes. Pride was evident that Europecoin had adopted the newest Bitcoin core codebase. Matthias Klees was quoted as saying:

"The OP is divided in texts for beginners and for professionals, to give everybody the change, to quickly understand the information, being relevant for his use-case."

September was a very uneventful month following on from the high activity throughout the summer. User "Limx Dev" kept publishing a list of who had received their new V3 ERC each and every Monday. Millions of new V3 ERC had been swapped.

At the end of September, Matthias announced the successful beta test of the "Term Deposit Enabled" Android mobile app wallet.

As shown on page 54, the Europecoin wall sign was incomplete in July. In early October, the sign had been painted and was ready to be mounted at the head office of operations. A photograph was taken at the time (see above).

On the 10th October, after two weeks of successful beta tests, the Android mobile wallet app was fully released. User "metamorphin" pointed out that the software was still experimental. He urged caution during the young development stage.

On the 19th October, an article was published on the news site called Altcoin Today titled "Europecoin... A Closer Look". It summarised how far the coin had progressed since being rescued in 2014. Reference was made to the creation of a new wallet client protocol and the subsequent launch of the V3 blockchain. Particular praise was given to user "Limx Dev". He had recently become the lead developer of Europecoin. The long term goal was written as:

"ERC was brought back to life for a cause. Matthias spent 5 years working as a consultant for some of the European Commissioners and their environment. In doing so, the decision was made to use what had been learned and the gained relations, to place a team of grassroots lobbyists for decentralization and blockchains in Brussels to influence politics. Matthias reports that even well-informed politicians have little chance of being independently advised without the influence of companies, and that these politicians are certainly interested in such an offer. The Europecoin website is designed as a management system for experts and expert groups and is equipped with individual options for activists and groups to actively publish about their work."

On the 22nd October, the market capitalisation of Europecoin (the combined US Dollar value of all ERC mined/staked to date) reached its 2016 all time high. According to www.coinmarketcap.com, the approximate figure attained was US$857,642. Daily trading volumes had significantly increased on the sole exchange on which the coin was being traded (Bittrex). A historical chart below displays how much the market capitalisation had ascended. It had more than tripled from roughly US$250,000 two days beforehand.

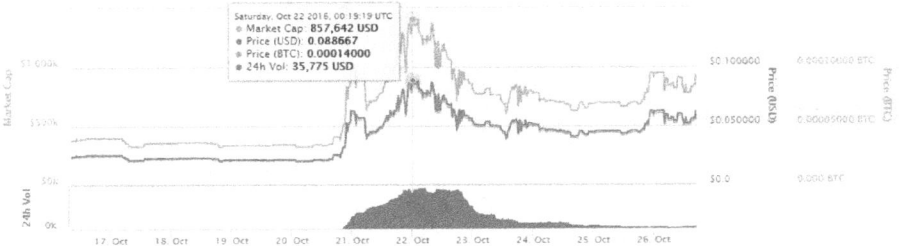

A higher market capitalisation was apparently recorded on the 22nd July at over US$8 million, but this was a miscalculation. The total number of coins had not been decreased, by a factor of ten, to ~9,600,000 ERC.

Sourced from www.cryptocompare.com, the Bitcoin Satoshi values of one unit of ERC account and total daily trading volumes (ERC) on Bittrex were as follows:

	Price	Low	Open	Close	High	Volume
18th Oct	3,496.5	3,258	3,617	3,376	3,617	9,947.32
19th Oct	3,437	3,436	3,436	3,438	3,438	5,779.36
20th Oct	6,670.5	3,258	3,353	9,988	9,988	268,877.64
21st Oct	11,394	6,300	9,988	12,800	13,680	540,207.10
22nd Oct	10.700	7,150	12,800	8,600	14,000	291,450.56

On the official Europecoin Twitter account, a Tweet broadcasted the moment the value of one ERC unit of account surpassed 10,000 Bitcoin Satoshi:

 Europecoin @europecoinEUORG · 21 Oct 2016
RUNNIG HOT snice 48h still increasing passed 10000sat NO DUMP
UNBELIEVABLE #crypto #fintech #SEPA #bittrex #altcoins #IoT #AMAZON
LOVING IT

On the 27th October, user "Limx Dev" reported that just over sixty five million old V2 ERC had been swapped for new V3 ERC. He viewed it as a great trust exercise between the core team and the rest of the community. He made it clear that the last normal swap would occur on the 31st October (Monday). It would become more difficult after that. He was confident that most users who wanted to swap had already done so.

On the 6th December, Matthias Klees and other associates met Andreas Antonopoulos, a Greek, California-based information security expert, tech-entrepreneur and author. He was made aware of the "Federated Blockchains Initiative" and given a related whitepaper. Europecoin awaited his feedback.

On the 9th December, a new promotional video for Europecoin was uploaded to YouTube by "Bitcoinsulting". It was given the title "Europecoin Decentralized Cryptocurrency Ecosystem". During the seventy five second long video, Europecoin is described as a stable, decentralised, modular cryptocurrency ecosystem. At the end of the video, a catchphrase read:

"Smart contract and service network without blockchain borders."

During the last week of 2016, two events took place:

- On the 27th December, version 3.0.2.0 of the wallet clients were released.

- On the 28th December, version 3.0.2.0 of the Android App was released.

Matthias Klees reiterated that EuropeCoin is a service driven project. He remained committed to develop and implement as many services as possible around the project, stay open minded and build collaborations with other crypto coins and blockchains in the space. On the last day of the year, the market capitalisation was roughly US$308,393 (1 ERC = US$0.031749 or 3,300 BTC Sat)

The last block timestamped to the Europecoin blockchain was:

Block #48,946 (Reward 1 ERC) December 31st 2016 at 11:53:54 PM UTC